IN MY DEFENCE

I HAD NONE

AAYUSHI LAURA

www.notionpress.com

Dedicated to the Tranquil seekers.

Preface

In My Defence, is not a structural poetry book but is a collection of loose poems that fits the theme of defending oneself, a search for something deeper—an attempt to make sense of the emotional weight I had been carrying. These poems are an expression of that search, a sincere reflection on the inner battles we all face, and a quiet exploration of how we reconcile with our own memories, choices, and contradictions. It is not about admitting defeat or claiming righteousness, but about understanding—seeing the full picture, even when it is uncomfortable.

This collection speaks to the depth of inner turmoil, the sincere yearning for peace, and the delicate process of detaching from the past. Each poem is a step toward self-awareness, an attempt to reconcile with the emotions that once felt overwhelming, and to find a sense of calm in the chaos. It is about recognising the impulsive actions and strong defences not as wrong, but as part of a larger process of growth—necessary steps in the path to understanding ourselves.

Through these verses, I sought to navigate the tension between self-justification and self-understanding, and in doing so, I realised that the process of healing is not linear—it is messy, uncertain, but necessary.

There is a depth to these pages that goes beyond simple reflection. It is about finding stillness in the midst of emotional storms, learning to let go of the need for control, and embracing the vulnerability that comes with true self-reflection. This is not a journey of transformation in the traditional sense, but of healing, of seeking peace and detachment from the turmoil we carry.

I offer these poems with sincerity, a touch of wit, and an open heart, hoping they resonate with anyone who has ever found themselves grappling with their own defences, yearning for peace amidst it all.

I

Never forced to compose as such,
The best poets wait to compose best verse.
A watcher of women or of birds,
Always knew the worth of time as much.

The strongest of monuments crumble,
If made to wait.
Legends pass on relying solely upon faith,
"And virtue is not virtue if he tumbles."

The lunatic was never as mad,
As society made of him.
Rebutting all the way, hardly ever glad,
In societal derangement filed up to the brim.

II

Hardly wrote about God, or religion,
About my spiritual beliefs or treason.
Never addressed him in first person,
Or thanked him enough for all that he gave me.
These religious beliefs fluctuate much often,
Depending on varying occasion,
But I do try to behold my faith and my vocation.

"So, how do you feel when people value you,
Or praise you in highest esteem?"
Taken aback, feeling numb, staring into spaces dumb,
Hardly ever knowing what to say,
"Casually try to soak it in
to motivate myself on dark days."
"But what about God?"

What an excellent question indeed, I ponder.
Probably should thank him more often, I wonder.

Performing pious deeds on pious occasions,
A devout of gladness might burst,
When the estranged child of the almighty rusts.
And my theocentrism often make steep turns,
Now and then when I try to find a way to earn.

So, I gave this question more thought
Than I had ought,
All these years, the things that were taught.
I should be more grateful for what I have got,
Hail almighty for this lot.

III

Spirits often take over my dozing mind,
Dreaming of things, pessimistically blind.
Playing with a double-edged sword,
Found dancing with the devil, never the lord.

Demons, Devils, and the Ghosts,
Hell-bent on staying, just until you are lost.

In the beginning of an end,
Or the end of a beginning,
The creator always stays ahead of its creation,
Things — I expect them to say at my cremation.

A head strong believer,
In a rut with my self-righteous soul
That hardly delivers.
And I hardly ever got a say,
As they comprehended my worldly decay.

Death awaits at my door,
Failing to catch a break,
Epiphanies of the shore.

Make it stop, take away these ghosts,
Snoozing and losing all that I have got.

And the night appears starless from my window,
Wondering, 'must be amazing to do starlight gazing.'

Laying still on the knocked-up ground,
Not so long ago, they took away my crown.
So, I lay down still, scheming to strike,
Plotting for a clean kill, with a sword or a knife.

A neat sweep, just a blow.
Maybe, just maybe then,
The night sky from my window might glow.

IV

Coward Robin, perched on a wooden moulding,
Flightless bird, baffling its foundling.
Whispering secrets, unbound to be known,
The Robin and the Nightingale, merely a pawn.

The listening moon never reveals,
As twilight weaves tales of their forgotten feels.
Each note a memory, each silence, a scar,
In the quiet of night, never flying afar.

And Robin dreams of skies, it cannot claim,
The Nightingale sings, unburdened by shame.
Two paths diverged, one lost, one found,
In the echoes of night, their hopes resound.

The wind carries whispers of forgotten lore,
Of wings that once soared but now touch the floor.
In the dance of dusk, where shadows creep,
The Robin struggles to take a leap.

A heart weighed down by remnants of sorrow,
The Nightingale sings for a better tomorrow.
For in every song lies a choice unseen,
To fly or to falter in the spaces between.

V

"I tried," said I.
Well, I didn't. I lied.
Didn't even want to. Why should I?

Forecasted a ruthless future,
As it was never in my nature,
To have loved and denied.

VI

The fumes and odour of the prior dates due,
Like flames to my fire renewed.
What baggage of emotions you intend to roast,
To burn me with them,
My beloved experienced ghost?

A bottle of wine much gracefully ado,
Cheap shots of what burden might do.
Derailing strain on a barren land with mine,
Holy Ghost stays evoked in the reverie of my mind.

Strained lips on frozen ground,
Frostbites redundantly persist,
What use be of this vain mind,
That forgets that you exist.

VII

What does the future behold?
What is their game?
Long alliances lost, never to be named,
And the truth about darkness must be told.

Serving defensive boundaries with colloquial rules,
What does my star sign say,
Do the stars align or are planning my decay?
Whatever was accomplished with spiritual tools.

How much will it cost,
A price, you must be willing to name.
As I rise to inexplicable levels of fame,
To fix all that I have lost.
Darkness of all sorts ruining my game,
Like a soon to be dead moth drawn towards the flame.

VIII

The legends I heard, all turned out lies,
Losers once, living best of their lives.
But hardly ever the above average child,
Whose parents had aimed for the centre with a dart,
With the hope that their kid might turn out smart.
How unfortunate they run down the streets,
Purposelessly — wild.

And the back benchers I find,
With generational wealth and zero minds.
With no talents whatsoever,
Their great-grandfathers still working together.
But really, how? Loss never acknowledged by that lot,
Me, I never came first, second being my favourite spot.

But who am I to rant? I have had a fair share of thrill,
Flights, and dresses, and charms.
And friendships, and glitter, and dance,
A decade filled with adrenaline and romance.

Yet envious with my debts and loans,
Of the gold I could never mine,
In a field filled with ashes, coal, and spurious dime.

IX

Only if I could kill a few,
When be that date due?
Not the only one who felt this way,
Demanding justice to this day.

And if I were to leave behind,
Some places and never find.
Strong enough to let grudges get old?
How they auction souls — sold!

Abusive and violent,
Exhausted, craving for silence.
What did they even get?
As I struggled to catch my breath.

Tattletaling all the way,
Grew up surrounded by drama.
Protection was just their excuse, I say.
Now, I seek validation for my traumas.

Am I strong enough to let it slide?
Do not want to run or hide.
If only I met them today,
Entrapped by these walls, waiting for decay.

I do try to hide my scars,
With a coarse smile, oh so dark!
And I just wanna run,
I have had just enough fun.

X

Regret the bizarre choices,
You had no idea you made.
Tirelessly dragging the man up the hill,
As you reach the peak,
Then and there, do you ever feel,
What could have been?

If it were not for this wolf of a man.
From the mountain top, do you ever feel the rays,
Hitting sunshine on your plenary door.
Forgot the promises you made to yourself?
Never wanting to stop, till the day you are dead,
Tough luck with these purgative voices in your head.

XI

Near the ocean by some faraway land,
Life rolling out exactly how I had planned.
Watching the sun set on that beach,
Vividly wrote down this speech —

"Always got what you wanted,
This privilege to you was certainly granted.
High time, the Phoenix must rise,
As you know about time — it flies."

Leaving behind the propriety, I once had in me,
Places, objects, people, and their love quick schemes.
On high road, wondering if life does me fair,
So, my soul doesn't end up crushed,
Like all my other affairs.

XII

Home was not a place on the map,
But a person for her,
Oftentimes poked about,
The delusion she labelled 'home.'

For all legal purposes and intent,
A brick affixed to another brick,
Is a young girl's prison,
And workplace for an older one.

And that was not what she had
Imagined her home to be,
So, she chose a person instead,
Not on the map but a place, that be kept sealed.
And never revealed for legal queries or such,
The bond papers they asked for,
Were always too much.

XIII

I found you or maybe you, I
Like rain finds the grass,
Amidst the cumulonimbus skies.

And it pours down my somber eyes,
Cause I found gold amidst brass,
On mogul grounds with magical ties.

XIV

Colourless green tides, eccentric frivolous schemes,
Unknowing what holds the future.
Or what the future holds, or deems,
Caressing with fury, a heartless creature.

Malicious intents via the devil's cradle,
On a rough ground with an unfenced stable.
Of hierarchy holding the utmost distinction,
Beguiling rounds with saturated concentration.

Meticulous and hampering, never meant ill,
Fearsome longings of grace turned evil.
As the coarse passage of time unfolds,
Undermined stories, caricatured to be told.

The gracious hosts of importance utmost,
Bequeathed by lies, betrayed by most.
Great demeanour, parental instincts unfold,
Tantalised with fear, stories untold.

XV

Unable to pull the trigger,
The paint paints my pain, all the feelings linger.
As I stick to a pen or a brush
Caressing enough, what's the rush?

If I could see his face once again
for the first time from a mile,
If only I could judge what's beneath that grin smile.
With whispers of soul burning emotions,
How much is too much
To set something epic into motion?

The rush, the blood flow, a solemn glow,
Hurdling through the veins, in one single blow.
Somehow, I resist myself at times,
To not pull the trigger,
Never even dared to cross the line.

The pen, the brush, or your word,
No less than a mighty sword.
Clueless, sane-insane,
The words of a poet always remain.

XVI

Much often, I deem myself unfit
For any sort of contact, touch
Or human relationship; causing pain
To my aching-numb brain.

Utmost sincerity seldom finds
Amidst all these bloodsucking hounds
I, a flea, or a tick. Not capable enough
To suck ample amount of red fluids.

So, I remain unstable and wonder
Will I ever achieve stability with the people
I cross paths with.

Certainty, my only resort, the sole affirmative.
Certainly, misfit for any relationship.
At least that is what I thought
Or what Kafka said he did.

XVII

How long before it all crumbles?
If something kills me,
Or if someone haunts me down?
The incessant mind,
Would never mind to drown.

But how far can I go?
With the burden on my shoulder,
Before I am hit by a rock or by a boulder.
How long before I bolt?
How far can I jolt?

And I have been told to hide,
Or in rituals my soul might get sacrificed.
For how long must I stride?
How many days left before I get immortalised?

XVIII

Thought I was immune to the paradigm of caste,
No one ever told me I could be discriminated against,
I lost.
Even in beleaguered times,
Hardly gave thought to such an obsolete matter,
Hence began the journey of my obliteration.

Heard many second or third hand stories,
Read history:
Was taught all about the shimmering glory.
Who knew it would come in the form it came,
Five years later — to this day, it remained the same.

I was informed,
It happened not because I was the centre,
But that is just how they intend to act,
Hatred, not for what I did
But for who I was — point blank,
Stared, had never heard stereotypes
Against our endeavour.

Who knew this could draw scars
On my oblivious chest.
Unrequited agony,

"Empathy for the ones facing expulsion,"
I had read.
Karmic kit in a circular fashion
Of all that has been done and said.
Never by me, but my kind.
Oh! For once let it rest.

Daring enough to not accept the wounds,
The *Incognito* that had me blown, didn't even found.
But I did no wrong or harm, a carefree child,
And it will always burden me so,
To live in such a toxic wild.

XIX

The chaser stops chasing
When the runner stops running.
And then their roles reverse
Continuing till affinity.

Gospel of sacred earth
Filled with countless mirth.
Never ending, human tendencies
To not settle for what they have got.

Until it's gone.

XX

Dancing on the gallows,
My pride, a hard pill to swallow.
A painter. A singer.
Unlike Freud, had no brains to fry.
A dancer. A player.
Dunks inside the basket on my very first try.

Betting against all odds,
A team player, no goals lost.
Acquainted to numerous languages,
A malignity, hardly recall any passages.

Taking care of all that I have lost,
A soliloquy for my ghosts.
Riding ponies on a gleaming sunlit coast,
Building muscles, I hated utmost.

"But we will get you presents
if you do well in academics.
Think it might be your forte."

So, I left it all behind.
Wondering what could have been,
Guess, we will never find.
In my defence I had what it takes,

Fair in every attempt I made.

But the burden of books,
Crumbled my jaunty talents.
Never ceasing to wonder what could have been,
As I punch the wall now,
With what we call a 'fragile fist.'

Foolishly, still wondering what I might achieve with
Milton, Pope, and Yeats in my league.

XXI

"Gifted with the face of an angel,
Fair, not too lean and beautiful,
But you could use an inch or two."

Miserable, if only I could beat my genes,
Growing insecure each time, I think.
But what about the genius I have?
What about my entrepreneurial skill set?

And the game gets harder,
Each time when someone's son or daughter,
Stand besides me, comparing our anatomy.
And these scars — just cause my inches could not par.

Disgusted by the ideology of ego and mellow.
What excellence is of use?
What beauty is to follow?
Absurd stance abused more than used.

"But everyone can't have everything,"
Petty defence for everything
That I could not be or think.
Yet, everyone questions the same,
To hell with her beauty or her brain,
When all this goes down the societal drain.

XXII

Fathers, like carbon on earth's crust,
A diamond or merely a peck of dust?
Dreadful dream of getting rust,
Daughters do try, put in them your trust.

Yet they hardly even try,
Righteously so, who are daughters to defy?
Wrongfully accused so many times,
Punished for countless things —
Not even their crimes.

So angry at their mothers,
"All you could find was this guy?"
Found '*Obituary*' relatable,
Disgusted to admit — they lie.

Try to ask for an apology,
I bet; they would not even try.
Righteousness ruling their head,
Will straight up deny.

Suffering daughters, all alone,
With mothers on the line.
No one to call home,

Forlorn creatures made enemies with time.

How simple it seemed,
Then the motifs of complications appeared,
Cause I loved him, and him I.
Yet his orthodoxy would never disappear.

Diamond, if only he had tried,
Relentless peck of dust
Made mud with teardrops on every cry.

XXIII

Gambled hard,
In the game of life.
You will find someone better,
Only if you tried.

What's love and honey,
Everyone's down for accounts.
Go secure life with money,
Your protector when in doubt.

All in all, money stays and love die,
So why marry someone poor?
At least, try to find a goldmine.
A gold digger in the making, they taught I.

Rigid, venomous, and vengeful,
Could not even deny.
Pathological pleaser of people,
Arbitrarily said I would try; I lied.

"No gold I would want,
That is not mine.
Join your forces blood-thirsty hounds,
Try to come for I."

Your poor upbringing, downhill went,
Trapped in a chamber, all left to die.
And we all saw them rant,
All your children sure did try.

Headstrong, fearsome, and wretched,
Wrong on so many days.
Yet never to wrong the man,
Gruesomely set in my ways.

A manipulative liar,
Could never put out my blazing fire.
"Money must be one of your top desires?"
"Well, my own gold in my own damn choir!"

Beware! Wrinkly old thief,
One day, you will be terrified.
Fearsome, and feisty,
You will be once and for all petrified.
When the time comes,
And the name is set in stones.
When I declare, what I did all along,
That day, you will get back what you've loaned.

XXIV

Where exactly did I go wrong?
Craved a beautiful life, not so long.
Sadness, a part of the process.
Why with sadness is everyone obsessed?

A life free of guilt, without locks on fire.
And who would ever choose me?
The one who owns the keys to my choir,
Could never afford to lose me, a duplicitous liar.

Someone who carries no shame,
Is not greedy for the covetous fame.
And I might as well throw myself at the wolves,
In the shadows, that's when they say the light pulls.

XXV

The stars all aligned for the betrothed,
Rambling around the couple of the hour begins.
Too special, pulling the A game, as the plot thickens.
Just ease her, she should't be this stressed,
Go please her.

Hydration goes a long way,
And her hairs should not be wet,
Running errands,
Facing the needles of derma's high-tech.
Overwhelmed she feels all day,
Shh… just catch up with her, you've got no say.
From managing to yelling at the chaos,
Freeze, standing still — getting lost.

Resentfully, looking at all that load,
Why is marriage such a stone pelted road.
As if a lane made of broken glass,
Oh! The horror to walk on it with dignity and class.

And a finger snaps in the air!
'Go fetch my brooch and that ruby clip for my hair.'
Running for life, taking part in all her affairs,
Doing the best, till she bids her fare.

And you certainly do not regret having said 'Yes.'
Until the vibe is off again,
And your head's again a mess.

But if it were about you, would they have helped?
And you know, I know it already
— The answer to that.
She chose you to indulge in her affairs.
But she no longer dwells there,
In parents' defence, she has had a fair share.

Mounted, lay your sleepy head
On her cumbersome lofty bed,
Where you have spent weeks,
Planning for a day she would end up getting sad.
Sacrificing your sanity
For someone you have loved and lost,
Rarely ever glad.

And she has been long gone now,
You were the best bridesmaid, knows the town.
A week later, a Thank you note comes in swinging.
That's when the bell tolls again in the head, ringing.

What would have been if you were her
And she was you instead?
And you know by now, we know the answer to that.
But I would rather stay delusional and play pretend,

'She would have been the perfect bridesmaid indeed.'
Cause she was my mural, my soul-sister in need.

But that ship has long sailed,
These thoughts often bounce back yet again.
Now that our paths rarely ever cross,
Now that she no longer misses me,
So much so for a loss.

I wonder what could have been,
If we still shared a mutual path,
And that is something I left for her to calculate,
Even though, I was aware she never loved maths.

XXVI

Forces of nature had all their hands joined,
As I made more money than all of them combined.

Never hid my shadow,
Longing for freedom,
Running down a meadow.

So, they casted spells on me,
Took refuge under a solemn tree,
Ousted I fell, bruised my knee.

Of light and of might,
Under the blanket of stars,
Moonlit kept me alive.

Wasted my breath,
And thoughts did count,
The lone wolf's decay, natures bound.

XXVII

Love, be not the spring or the sun-kissed noons,
But the storms of winter and the thunder of monsoon.
Always meant to arrive in a full-fledged package,
Not just the sunny parts, do claim the whole baggage.

XXVIII

Never forgo, how much I root for you,
How I pray for your well being.
With a wish — you roar like a lion and win,
Not to forget how much love I carry within.

How I hope we be the only duo, snarky enough,
Despite life, that's been rough.
Do put a gold lock on your brass-plated gates,
Our faith, strong enough to shake tectonic plates.

How on earth, were you and I linked,
I wonder what exactly did God think.
Surely, he knew they would kill together.
And our arsenal could not even tether,
Like two different birds in a flock,
With matching feathers.

XXIX

The toughest thing you had ever done?
"Begin from the beginning and never run."

XXX

"No amount of hurt or pain
or wreckage or disdain, I could bestow
in me with the hopes and dreams
for you to guilt me of shame."

Your troubles always greater than mine,
And I, never troubled enough
To understand your verse or your line.
The load I carried for a glimpse of your smile,
Guilty as sin, mistakes of my brain senile.

And you would never let go…
Anyhow, I had forgiven
The greatest of sinners and their crimes,
Go ask the world about the suffering that was mine.
And my friends all warned me as I crossed the line,
Ebbing and flowing composing emotional fables,
Scheming lower and lowly around the sorcerer's table.

And you danced under the moonlight once,
How beautiful for such a tramp your efforts and love.
Until you declared it a mishap,
Something you would always regret.
What a shame, the scrutiny of your pain,

In disdain, yet again.

Once upon a cynical time,
He aged like the finest of wine.
And I did my best, so I will just let it rest.
As blur as the memories I bury,
The love never load-full to carry.

XXXI

If I could go back in time
To the thirteen years old self,
The person I needed then, that I was at nineteen
To tell her what to be.

If I could go back in time
To the person I was at nineteen,
The person I needed then, that I am today
And tell her what not to be.
She must have felt safe and seen,
A budding spirit with untamed choices.

And now I wait, for the thirty years old me,
To teach bravery to this condescending soul,
To help her through quarter-life crisis,
And to help achieve her long-lost goals.

XXXII

Staring into nothingness, gaze the second's hand,
Every second it moves, an airbus lands.
Vain relinquishes with pity glare,
Yet again failed, to make an itinerary for somewhere.

What if someone kills me, as I sat and stare?
None could rescue, thus ending all my affair.
These walls built for my protection,
What if they couldn't protect me?

So, just in case if I die today,
Bury me with my songs and a rifle,
Let the winds carry whispers of my fight,
Of battles lost, with dreams that I held on tight.

In the earth, lay my weary soul to rest,
But let my spirits rise in the songs I've confessed.
And if you come to visit, bring no tears or sighs,
Just a smile for a soul who dared to enjoy.

And if you find my force drifting apart,
Know that I sought the light in every scar.
Just bury me with my songs and a rifle in my hand,
A soul unyielding, forever seeking new land.

XXXIII

"Just for a night, let's not fight"
Shut the demons in my mind.
Words gone vague; soliloquy indescribable.
Word on the street; "She's turned insufferable."

XXXIV

Wanted daffodils on a pretty string,
Make a crown and take a swing.
But you got me a sunflower,
Which sure does twinge.

Wandering around in the field,
Wishing I had gotten daffodils instead.
Romanticising them the way romantics did,
Near the lakes, never to get rid.

The mogul in my heart seldom sighs,
As daffodils blossom under the scarlet sky.

XXXV

Easier said than done, never met someone,
Who felt the way I feel.
Mechanically working, hardly ever thinking,
Accepting my fate, crossed enough to lose all faith.
Want to turn things around, drop it,
Go touch some grass, just stop it.

The mountains I carried,
That were only meant to be climbed.
Time to lose the baggage,
Relentlessly, dragged around in a carriage.

Thought of dancing with the devil,
Drew blood – unleashing darkness of the evil.
Strikes midnight, thought of doing well.
Dread falling asleep or eat or think,
Laying down, lost — I sink.

No sounds audible of the Devil screams,
Must be why one should not daydream.
Excruciating burden, to be carried around in a plate,
Mayhem, Lucifer sealed my fate.

XXXVI

My love won't ever come to an end,
Very first friend, with her whole life I did spend.
And a layman could never comprehend,
A lady of such demure.

Except for one, her own flesh and blood.
And she may have told me once or twice,
There was flood when I opened my eyes.
And the mythology stands corrected,
the clouds bawls their eyes out,
With thunder-like screams, so loud,
For the birth of greatness, of stature, or demeanour.
So, I led a life living it, I — a hopeless dreamer.

'For you I would kill,
You, my sole reason for this footlong thrill.
My child, spread your wings — just fly.
Fly as high as your hopes deem,
Be unstoppable,
Measure the earth In one single beam,
Never let anyone crush your hopes or your dreams.'

XXXVII

A month passed since you left,
Can't seem to catch my breath.
All the long calls and dreams we share,
Can not withstand how much I care.

And you took some losses I heard,
That's just how you get your life figured.
And father never puts you on the grill,
Life ain't the same without that thrill.

He roasts me, I tell you
Morning, noon, and night,
On most weekends, we surely do fight.

But nothing has been the same, since then,
Just know that I will always pine for you.
However, whatever it is that you are doing,
Fine for you!

XXXVIII

Craving for a place unknown.
Soul bequeathed; life unborn.
Standing still amidst the crowd,
Demo-phobia screams aloud,
Irony of life bursting my bubbles and clouds.

XXXIX

In shadows deep, stringent prophecies lie,
I tread a path where envy's gaze is keen.
Each step I take, a watchful eye,
The plots unfold in silence, cold and mean.

Cursed with glances sharp as winter's bite,
With schemes like shadows stretched to stay.
And I perceive their malice in broad daylight,
Yet, no strength found to push the wrath away.

The weight of disdain grows hard to bear,
Their hidden hands impede each forward stride.
I strive in vain, caught in their darkened snare,
A battle fought, many a soldier with weakness died.

And I see their spite and feel the strain,
I struggle on, though the progress struggles in chains.

XL

This cage was just fine a while ago,
Storms often cloud my judgement as I go.
Neither urges felt nor the need to grow,
I want whatever I can have,
Whatever I can get; just give up and bow.

Neither lines drawn nor bounds known,
Do not want the clout.
Whatever the mind emancipates,
Would want without a doubt.

Things influential had never influenced me so.
This cage that seemed just fine a while ago,
Has begun to drain my girlish glow.

So, I plan and plot of breaking free,
But where will this bird go?
Never nested another tree.

No helps to seek, was never really weak.
And pleasing tendencies die hard screaming,
Pleasing harder, buying a golden cage, still scheming.
A sadist lion, and a masochistic lamb.
What a brilliant pair indeed.
Dear Valour, where are you when I need?

XLI

Nemesis, Oh! Nemesis, my nonchalant lover.
Claiming forces with wretched smiles all summer.
How high were you to make such an unworthy choice,
What was it? The work, the test,
Or her high-tech device.
Forbidden glimpses, burying hearts fragile.

God forbid, I admit the rush,
But my oh my! It just ran so deep,
You had me crushed, could barely sleep,
In my mind fairy lights, our spark so lit.

And I gave in more thought than thoughts required,
Why couldn't you just admit that you got tired?
When I made fun of you,
You laughed, but your laughter ruined me.

She won you over whilst I played on your team,
Only to find that you loved to play alone.
Deranged by the girl, my benevolent nemesis.
She found someone better,
At least, that's what she thought.

But to tell you the truth, you could have just tried,
Unaware to this day, ungrateful nincompoop, you lied.

Coarsely unaware, finishing adventures and dares,
Just wonder what we could have been,
Only if you were fair.

This curse I bestow, for you to admire,
You could not abide by the rules of this tryst.
Nemesis left, long gone, but you were merely a liar.
What stays is an underlined red list,
With your name in it.
In my mind fairy lights,
Yet our sparks never caught fire.

XLII

Because he loved me more,
His eyes were always sore.
And I loved him just as much,
Yet his derangement demanded pain as such.

XLIII

A poet or a poetaster, let's roll and see the times twist,
Playing with words like fire,
Hold down my composing fingers or my wrist.

Sincerity and rhythm sit in a corner and cries,
Ink bleeds, my brand-new ink pen quickly dries.

Rarely caring about the meter, my verses run blank,
A liar or a cheater, behold my rank.

Much influenced by Pope and all his pranks,
Care to share how high was he,
Or what potion he drank?

XLIV

Wonderful things told, of you now and then,
But I did not wish for this, passion's praise.
Coaxed myself I am better off,
Sane-insane, just crack the joke.

Go on, come on look alive!
Tell them of the adultery
You carried around in a drive.
Random tears cloaking the sight,
Just because you strolled away from my light.

Farce or satire, with a hoaxing desire,
Rust on a metal clamp, much less admired.
But what should one label a bully?
Not my narrative, signing-off duly.

XLV

Longings of freedom, to fly and never return.
Down too soon? How can one learn?
When it is better to have found the one,
In a world filled with crap, roam until done.

Oh! Beloved entrapment, bittersweet strain,
Your pain, a paradox I cannot explain.

Too blue to regain the conscious and the worldliness.
Loved by a few, crushed by one,
Pedantry circumstances, seen by none.

Oh! How benevolent your spirit has been,
Nowhere to be found or to be seen.

XLVI

Whatever happened to the fun and games
Children used to play in schools.
The groups of boys, and trios of girls
They were happily all fools.

Whatever took place in those corridors
Remains a secret, not yet in a deep rut.
And then it came — the age of rebellious youth
With the traumas we all rant about now.
Finding our true selves
Everything passed on — not too well somehow.

And no one will ever find out
Whatever happened to those smiles.
The petty rivalries, the class-room drama
And the basketball trials.
And the teenage schemes, as we know them now
Came in from the last of the benches.

Uncertain of the whereabouts of those schemers
Bet they all got out of their scheming
And are now dreamers.
Who's ever gonna invest in their troubles and trauma?
It all seems illusional

As I strolled down the carefree streets of Roma.

But we all grew together, knew so much better
Had the zest to fight and unite.
Yet it all went away just like that, one night
And all our hearts did shatter.

Who is to say what we are anymore
If we are living or just surviving as we grow.
Some might even wonder of my whereabouts
May nostalgia hit them just as hard and loud.

Whatever happened that broke their hearts
The happiest faces got the most hideous scars.

They were once all small, carefree, and fine
Some bullies, some oh, so divine!
Now the twenties hit some twisted nerves
Who is to say, what is this thing called love?

Yet, what hurts the most stays unspoken.
And none will try to pull back the curtain
To find what was it that wrecked me, ascertain.
Neither I, of them, all too broken.

And just like that, everything ended
Friendships once broken could never be mended.
But I still wish, to be missed just the same

Only if I could tell them
I miss them more than I claim.

XLVII

Better than thousand forces combined,
In grandeur, egos all intertwined.
Working like an ant, never whined,
Looked him up, blissfully divine.

Oh lord! So beautiful.
Careless creature, a slave of time.
Winning the hurdles, crossing the line,
Swallowing pride, trying just for the sake of trying.

Money and honey on the same table?
Old sagas hardly ever find.
If only I could sink and drown and die
In the musings I write.

With all heavenly forces combined,
A slave of hell, yet never did he mind.
Blissfully him and I, were
Metaphorically conjoined.

XLVIII

Mind glitched, as I thought of you,
A friend? Maybe, but let's re-examine your lot:

Ringing in very first call,
When you want to share all that, you can recall.

And I had heard Shadwell was dull,
But somehow you managed to outdo him.

Laying idle, dumbness becomes you and grey you have
already been,
Showing care when care is nowhere to be seen.

Never with the poker face, your eyes so easily swell,
Still a flatterer when flattery could have you sell.

XLIX

Butterflies for the make believe
Pillow-talk that I had with you tonight.
Sleep talked dreaming of a beautiful life.

Longing for the water sprinkles
And the fluids, as I purposely bid you fare.
Made aware by the delusion of darkness
And the dark desires of your righteous soul, so bare.

Flummoxed with the awareness,
We are better off ceased.
Yet you talk to me most nights
Just before I am off to sleep.
Signing off, I must meet you now in my dreams,
With water in my eyes, sliding off to where it gleams.

L

In my defence — I had none.
I grew because of the blood I drew.
And with all the powers vested,
This wish to me was granted.
And just between me and you,
The greatest poems of all time
Never on a paper landed.

www.ingramcontent.com/pod-product-compliance
Lightning Source LLC
Chambersburg PA
CBHW031803150726
47989CB00006B/2856

डॉ. बारबरा सभी बीमारियों का इलाज

एसटीडी, एचआईवी, कैंसर, हरपीज, मधुमेह, स्तंभन दोष, किडनी/लिवर रोग, गठिया और कई पुरानी बीमारियों के लिए चरण दर चरण सिद्ध बारबरा ओ'नील सिद्ध प्राकृतिक उपचार

एल्मर होश

Made with ♥ on the Notion Press Platform
www.notionpress.com